Welcome
to
Color Me Botanicals III
An Adult Coloring Book

Please visit our website for more information on new designs, books and available matted prints at
www.botanicalartdesigns.com

ISBN: 1511878851
ISBN-13: 978-1511878852

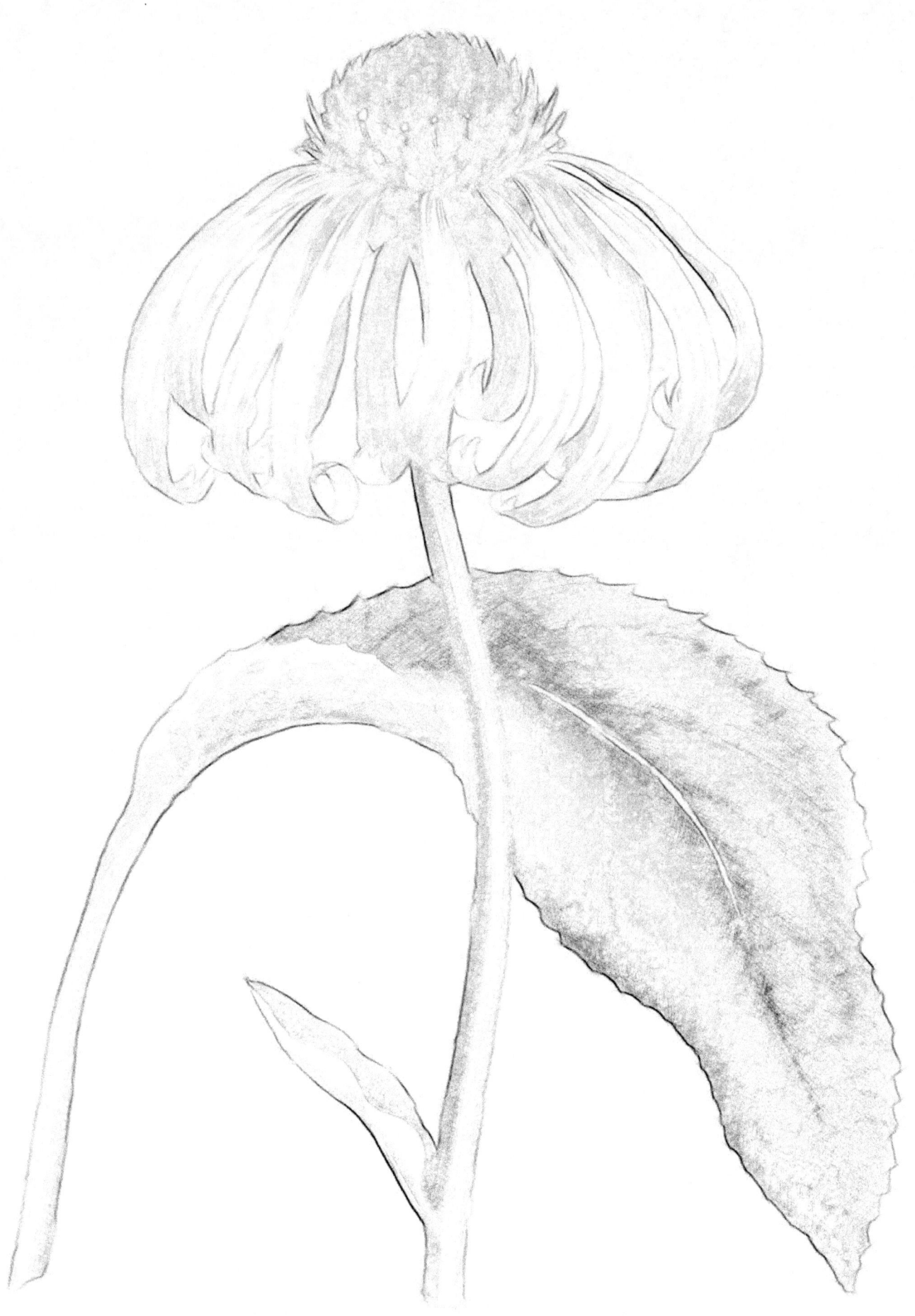

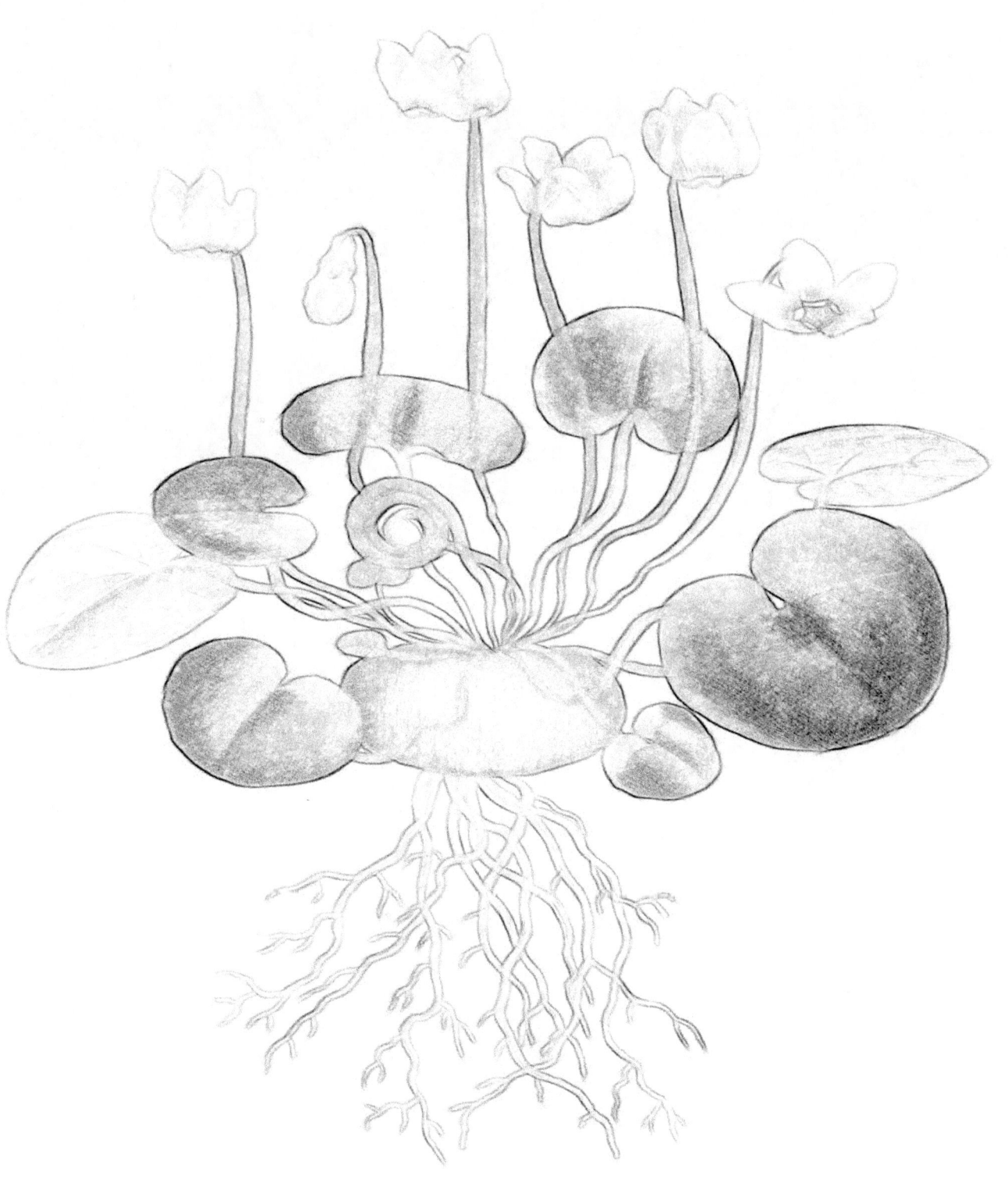

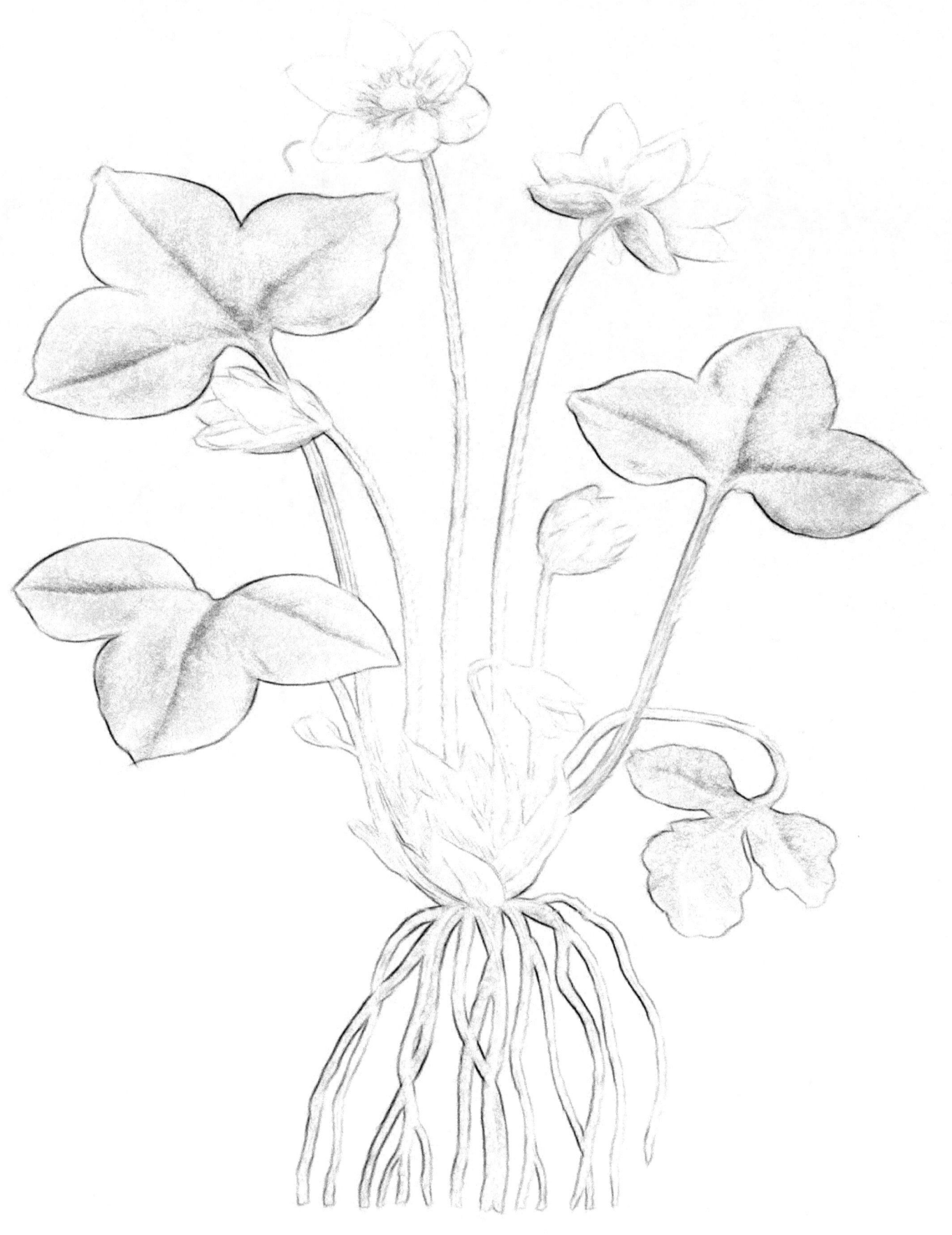

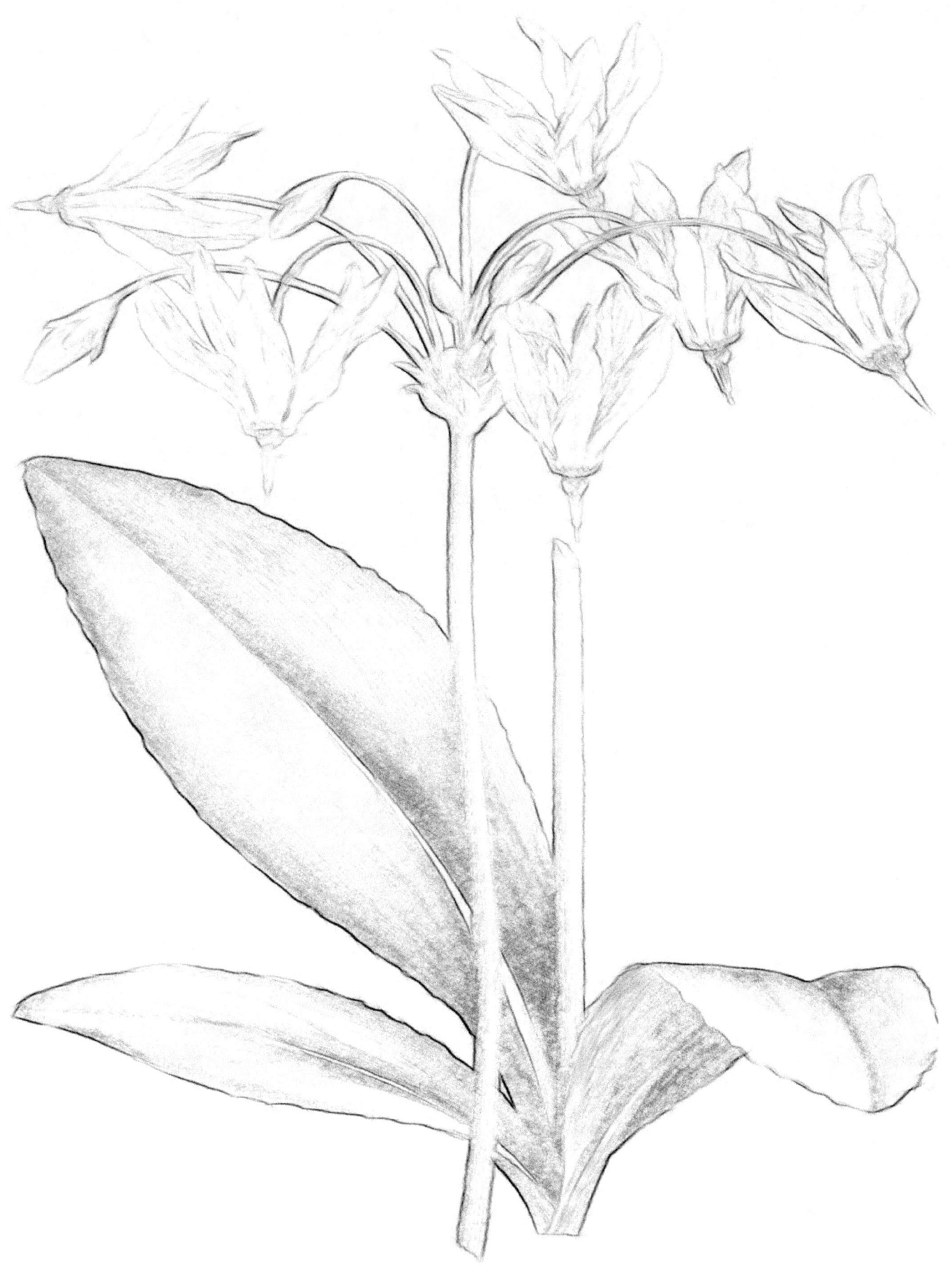

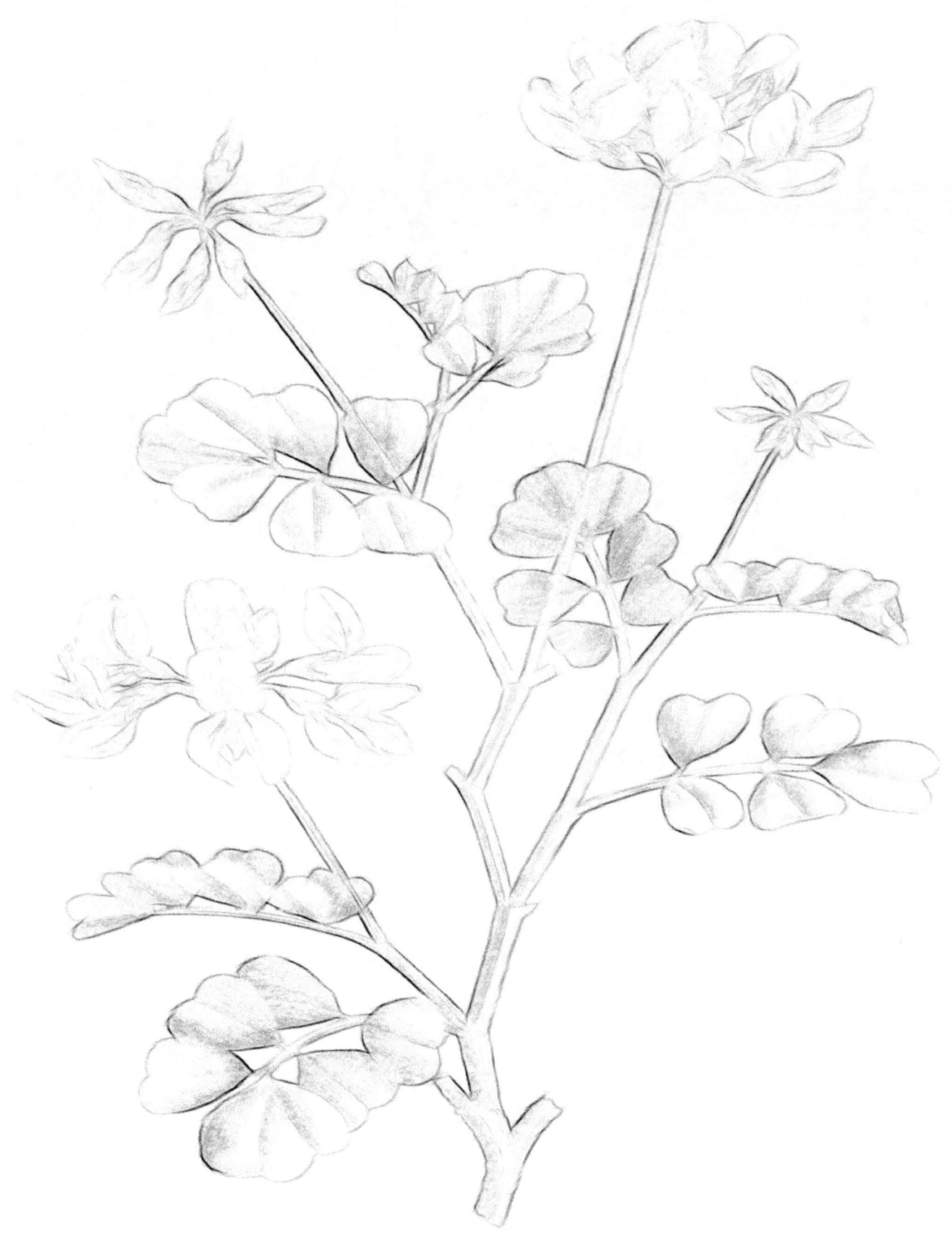

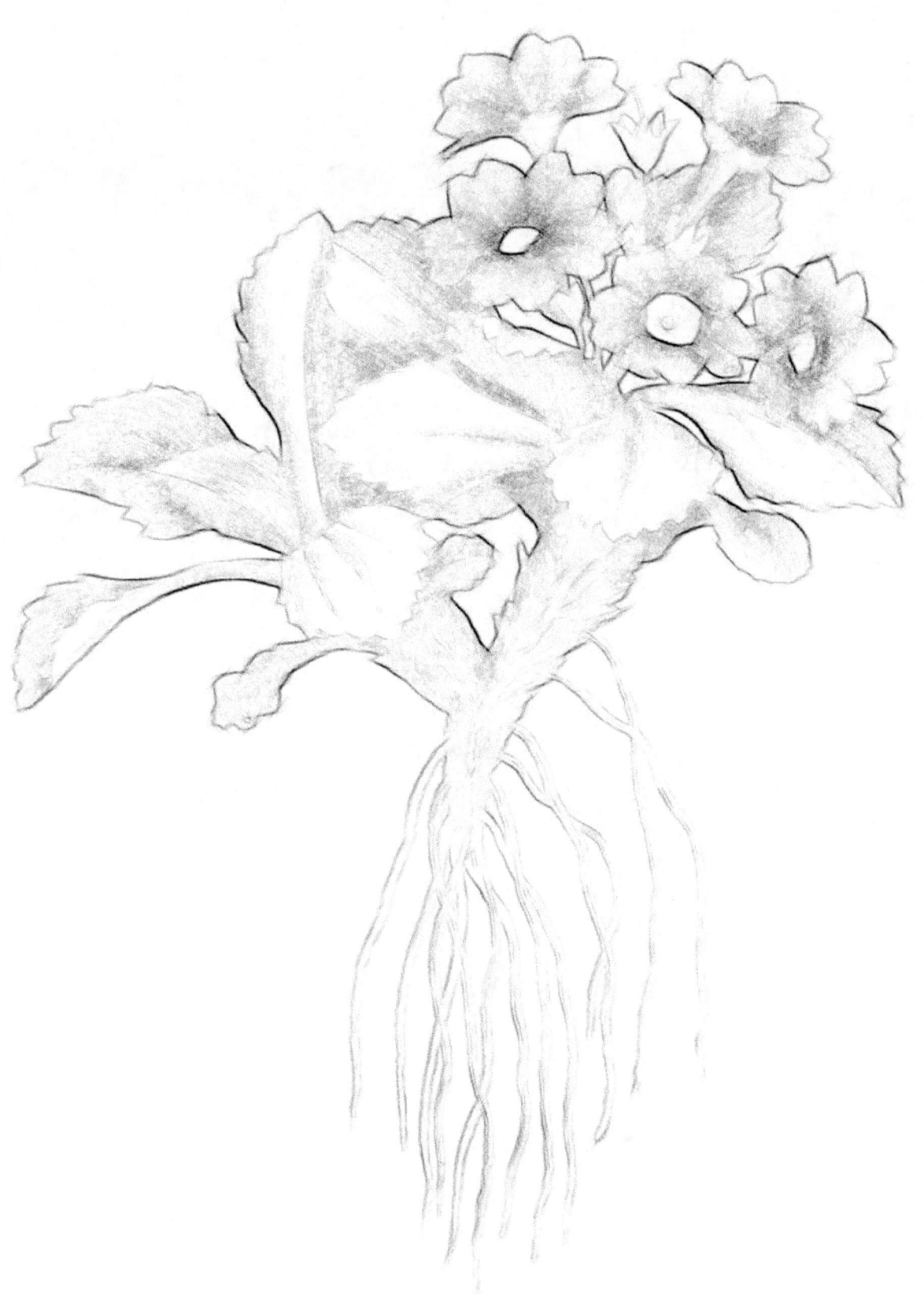

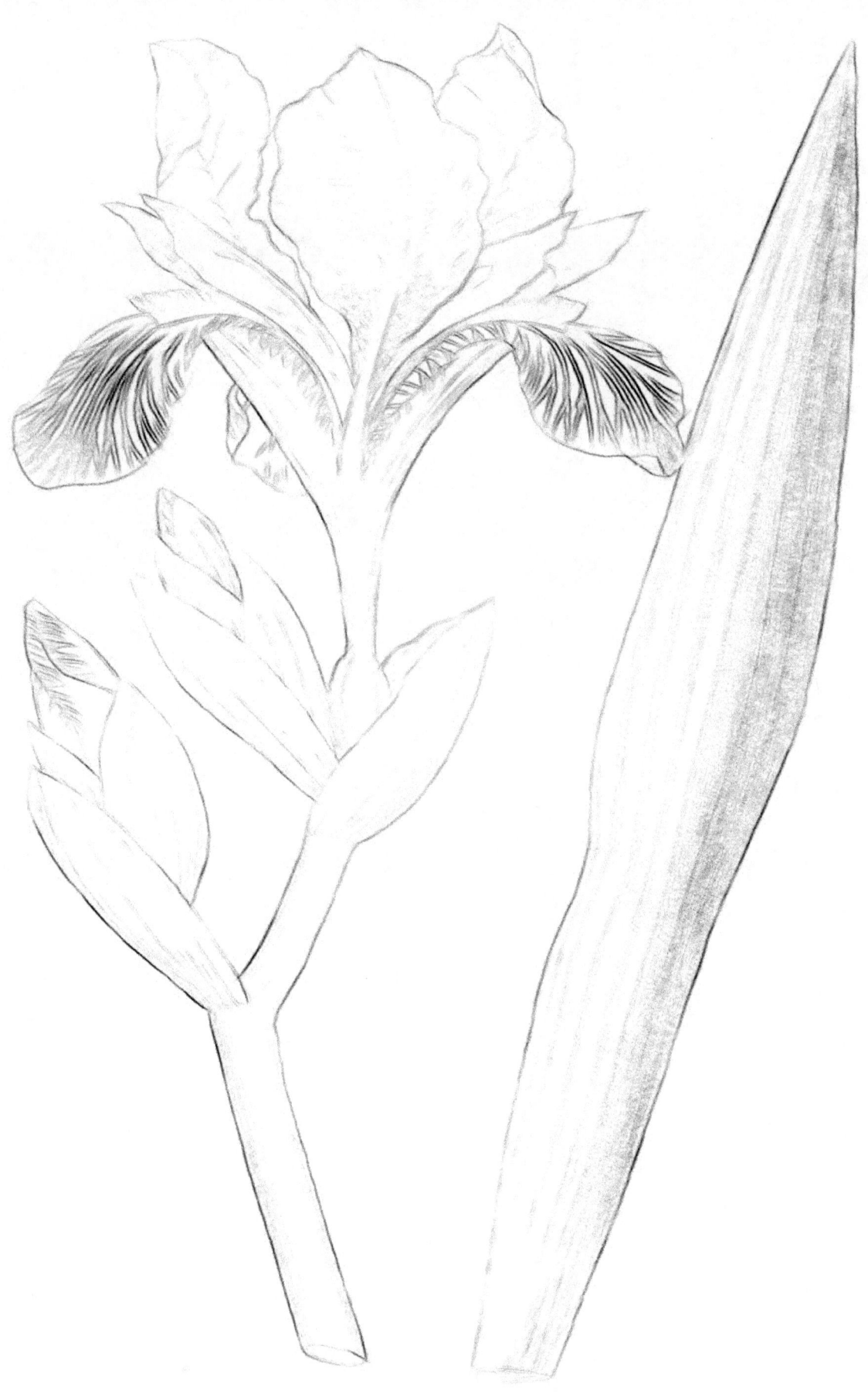

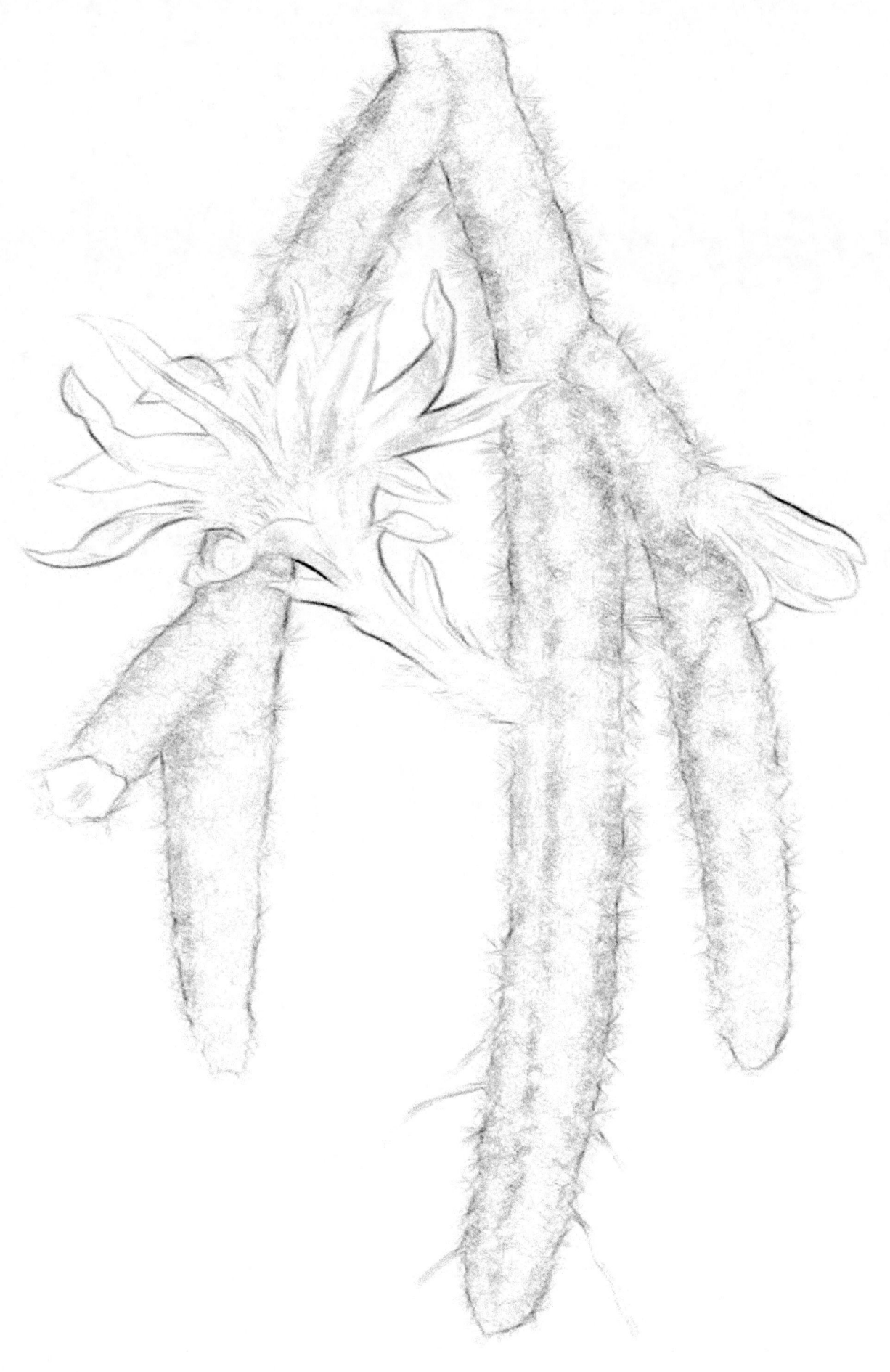

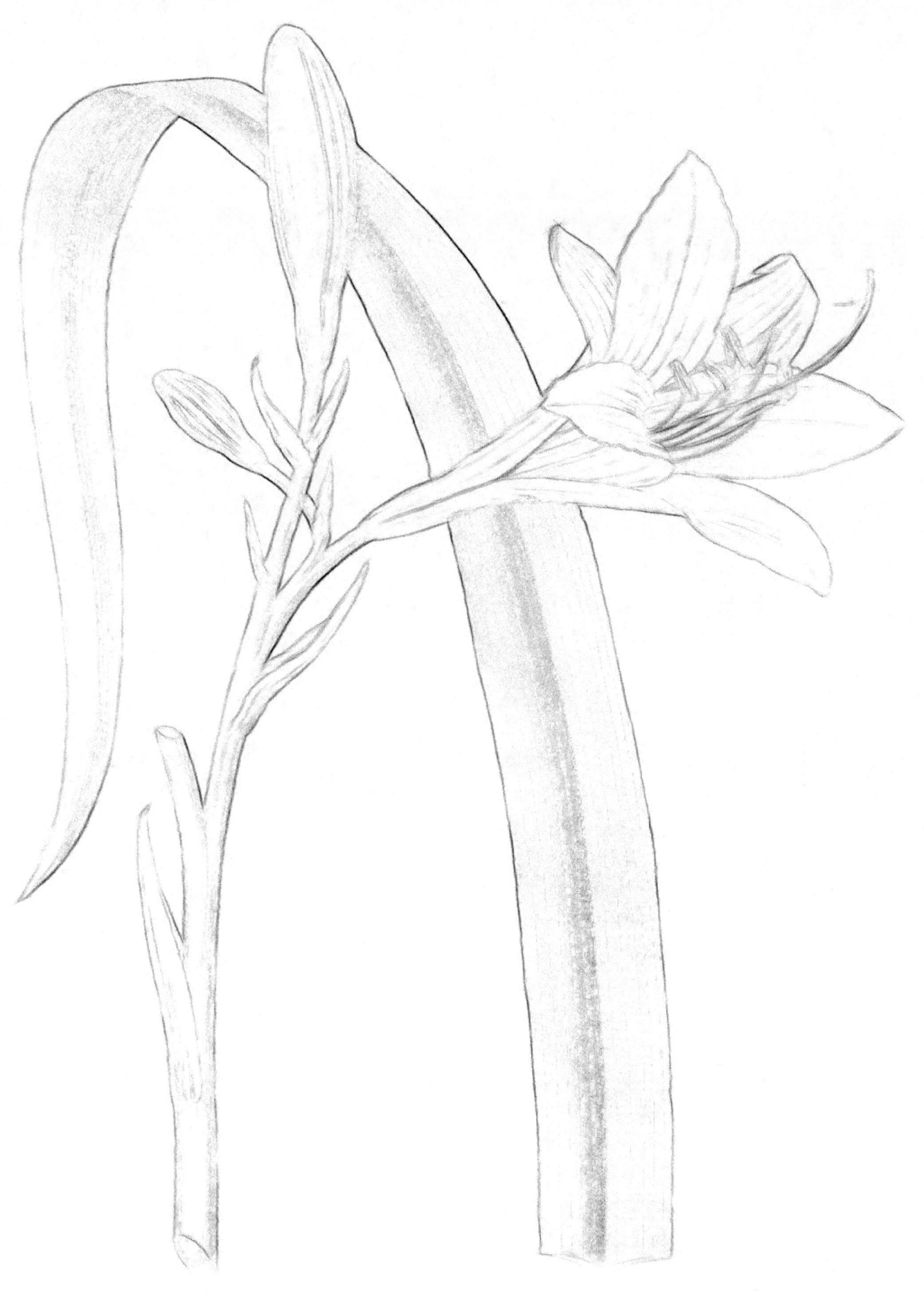

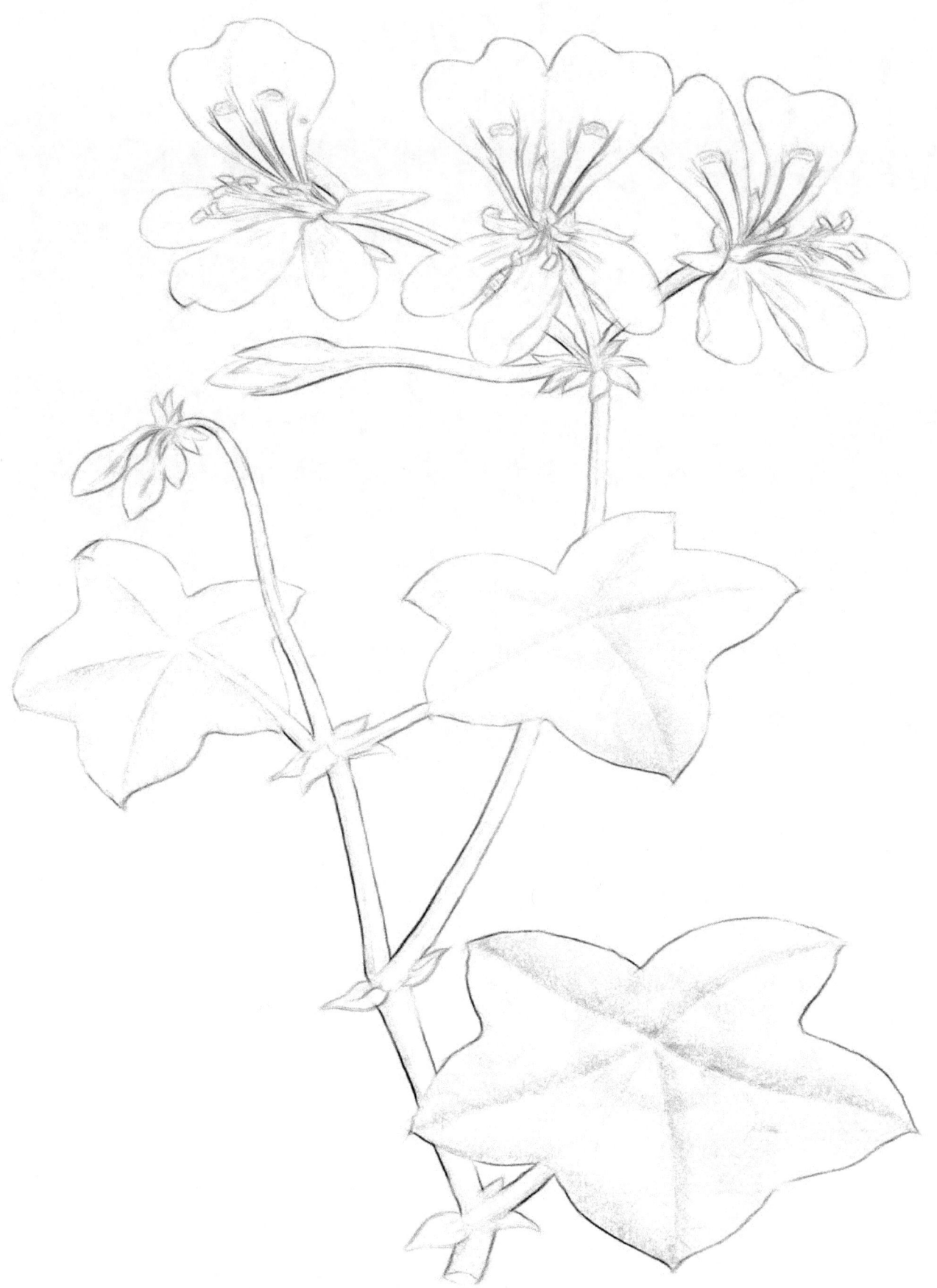

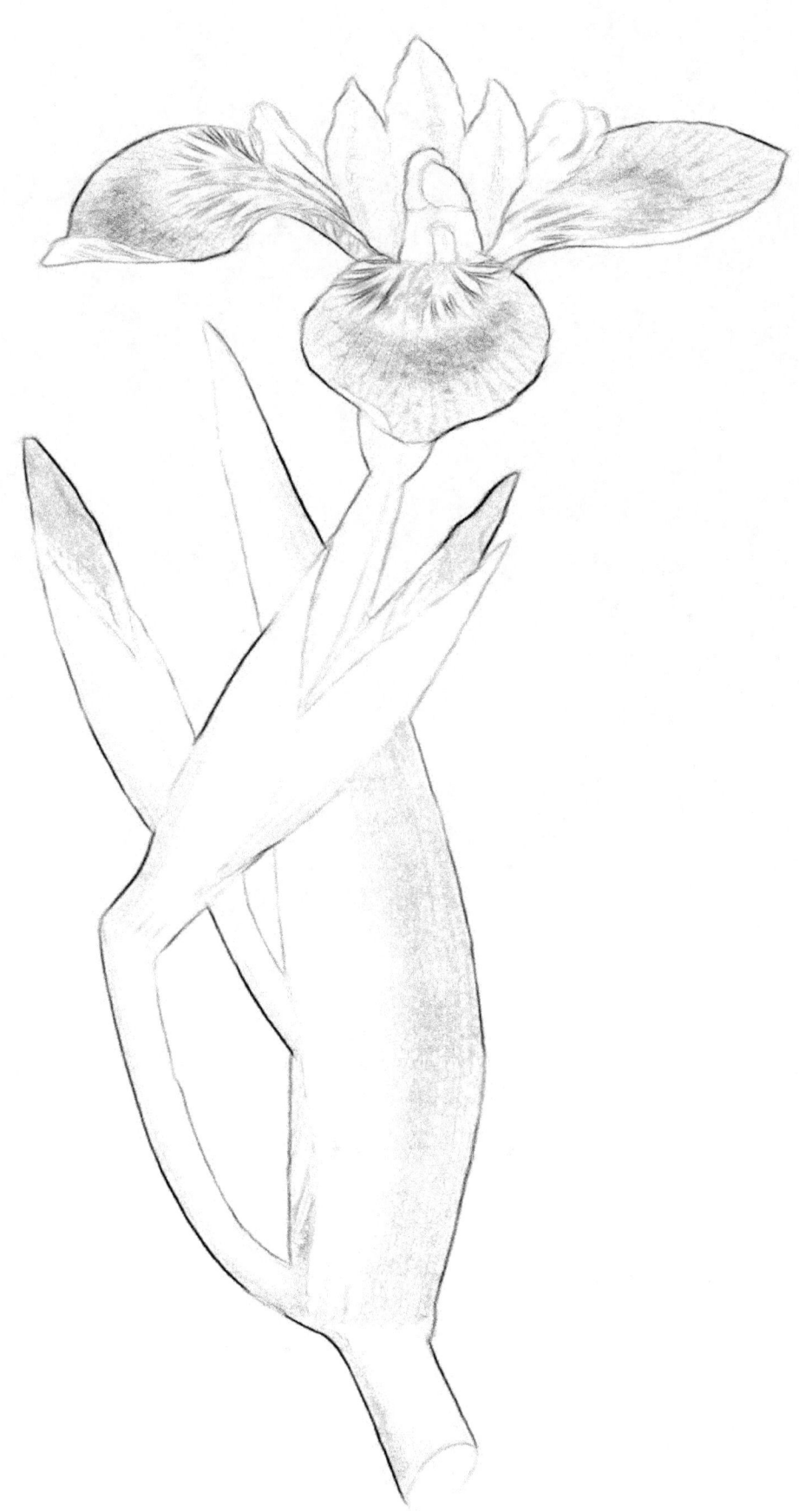

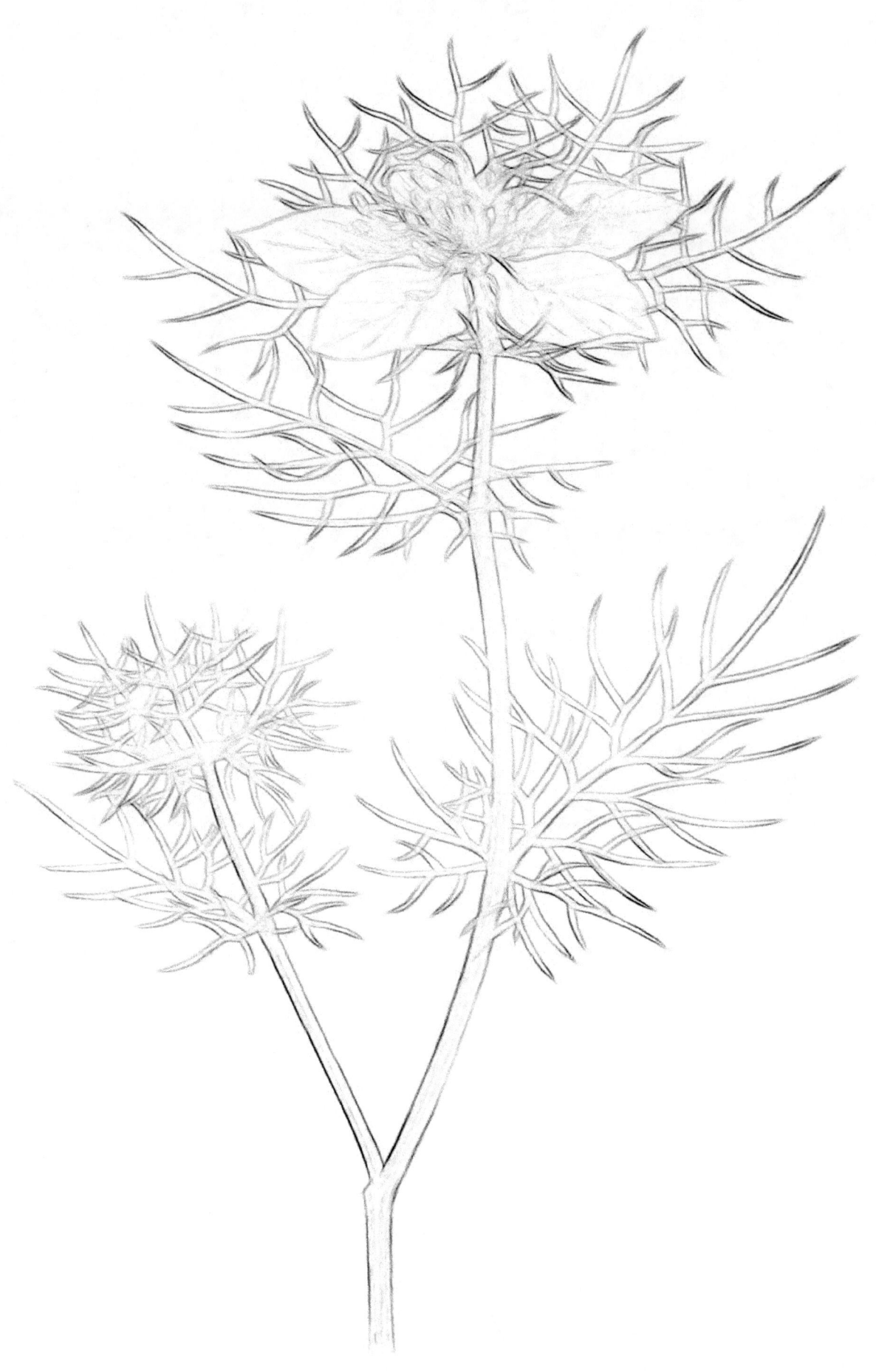

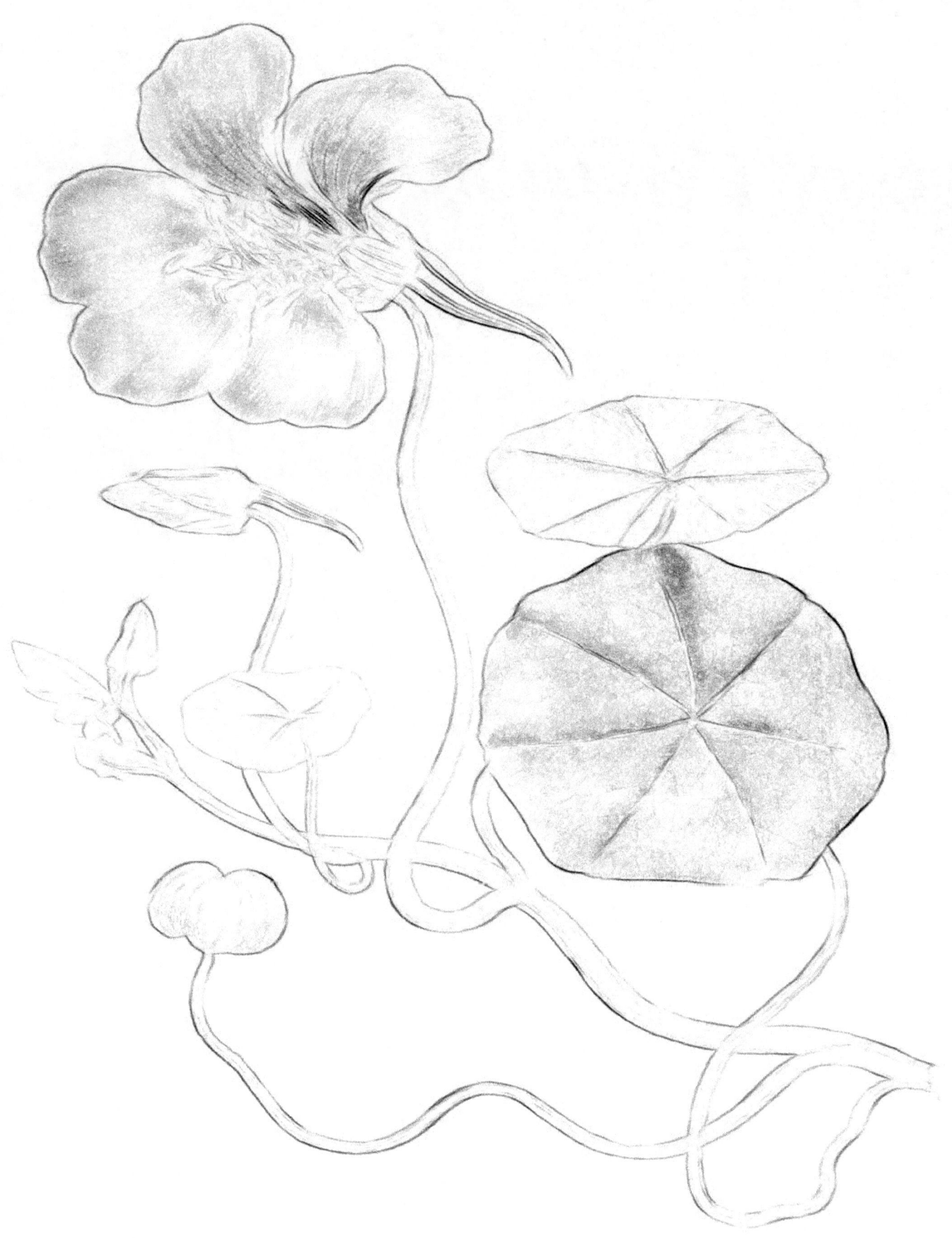

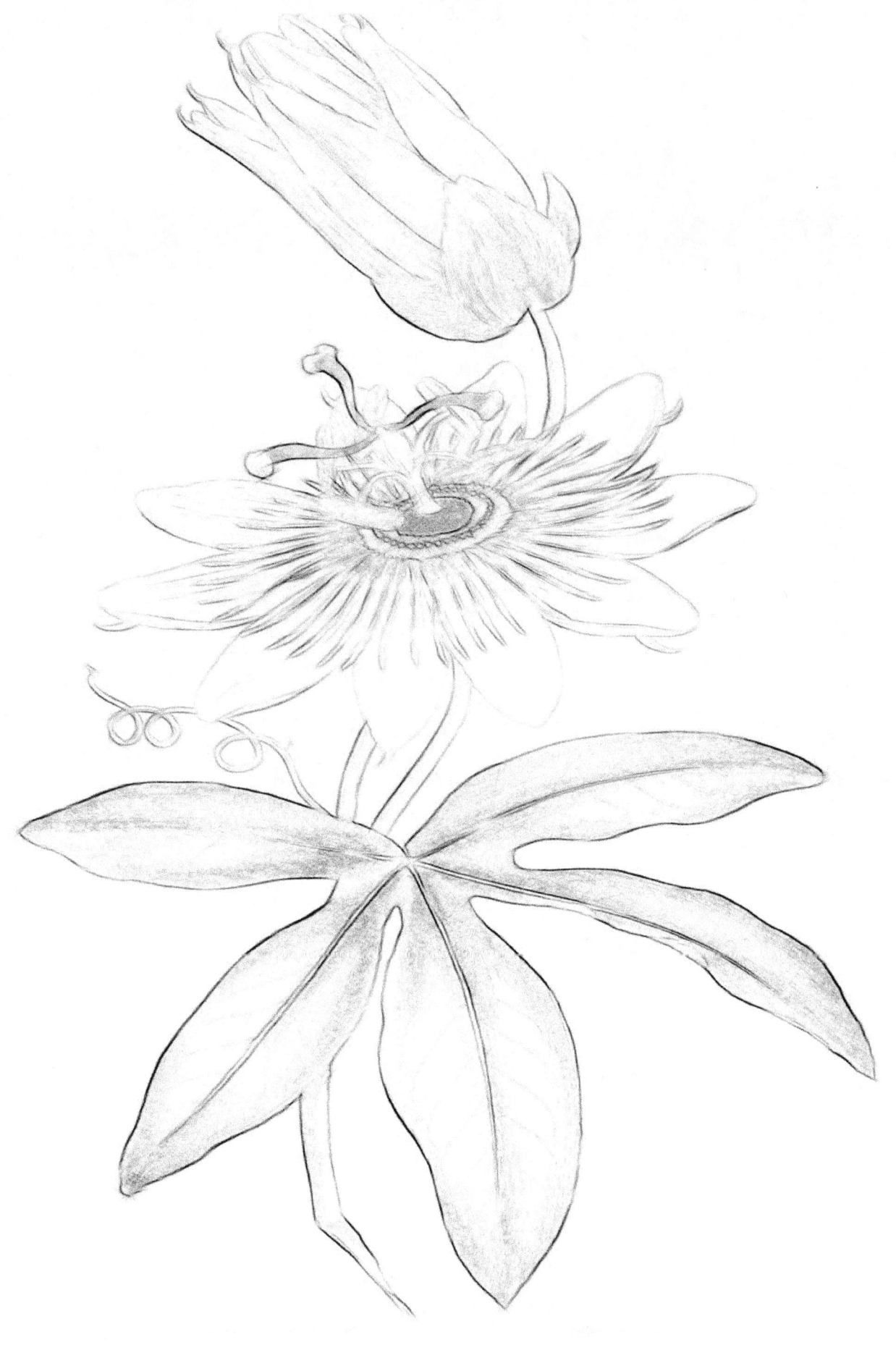

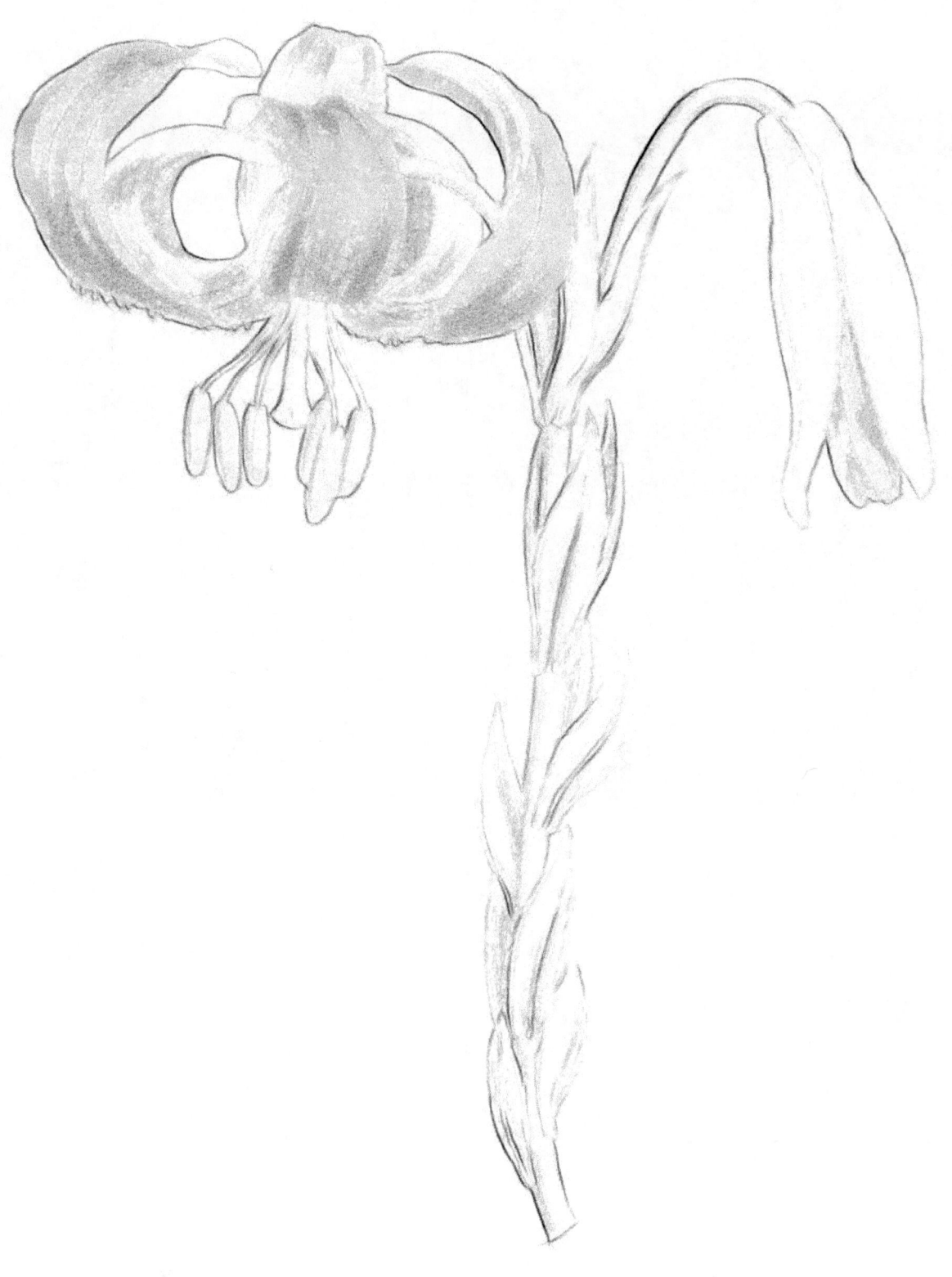

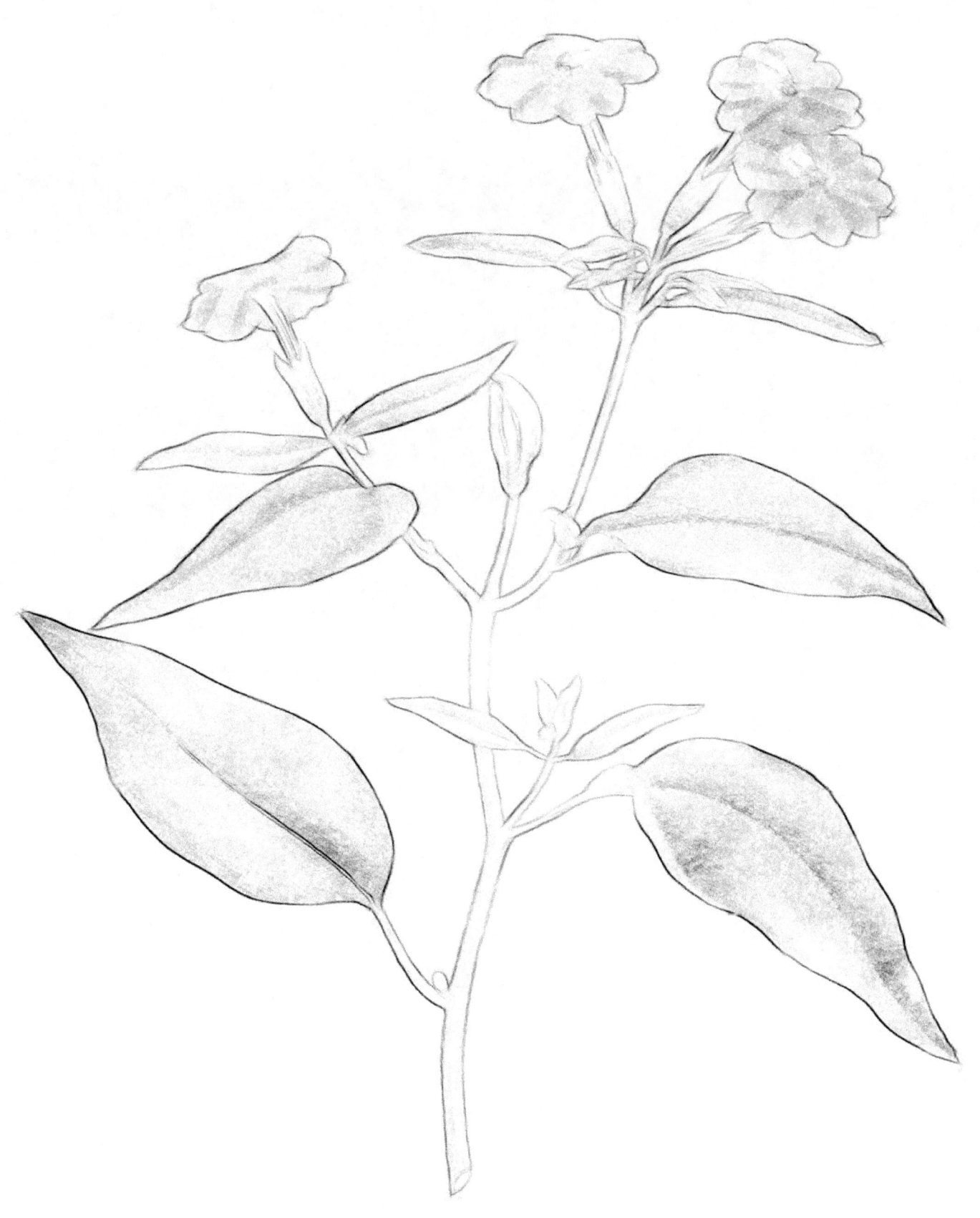

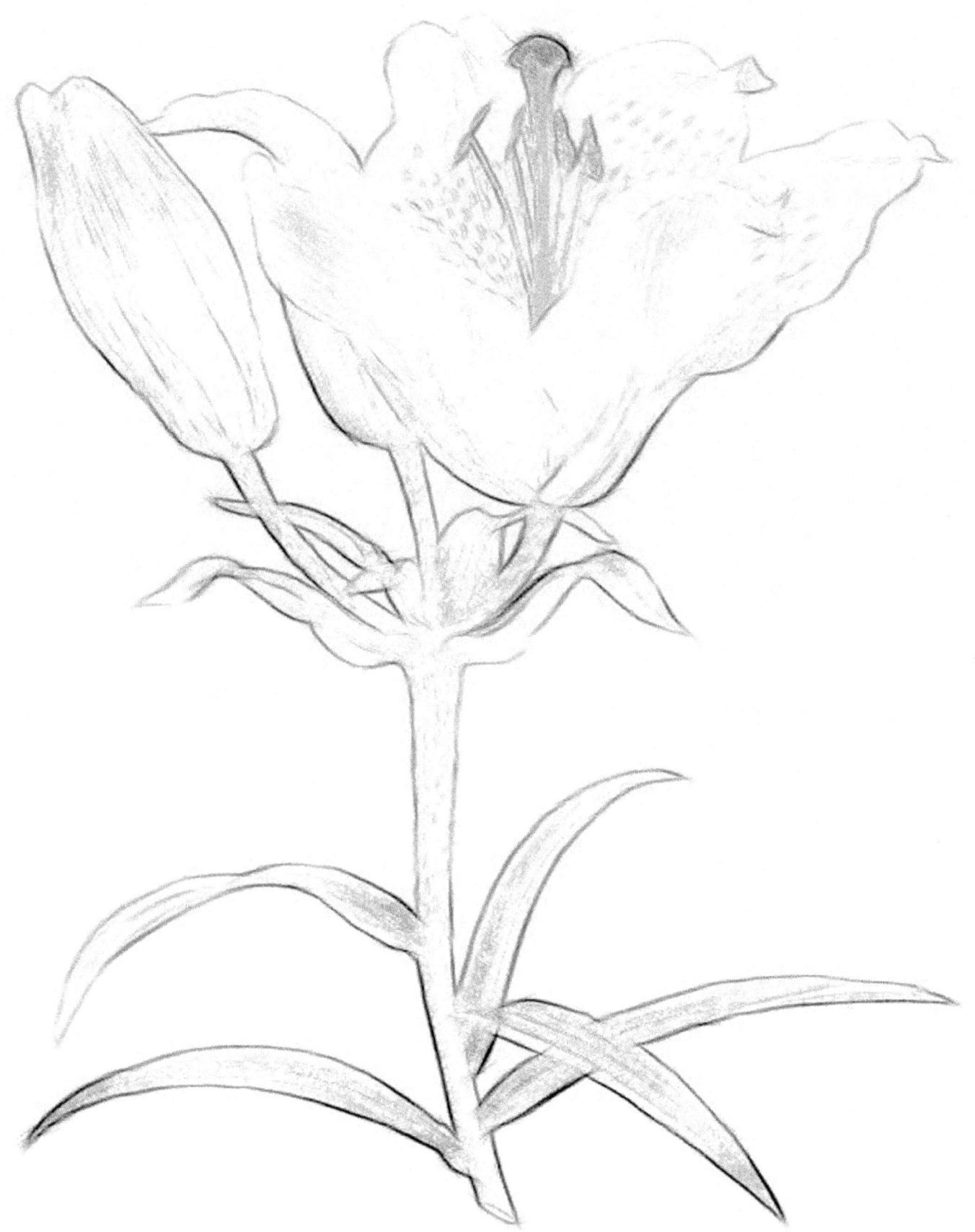

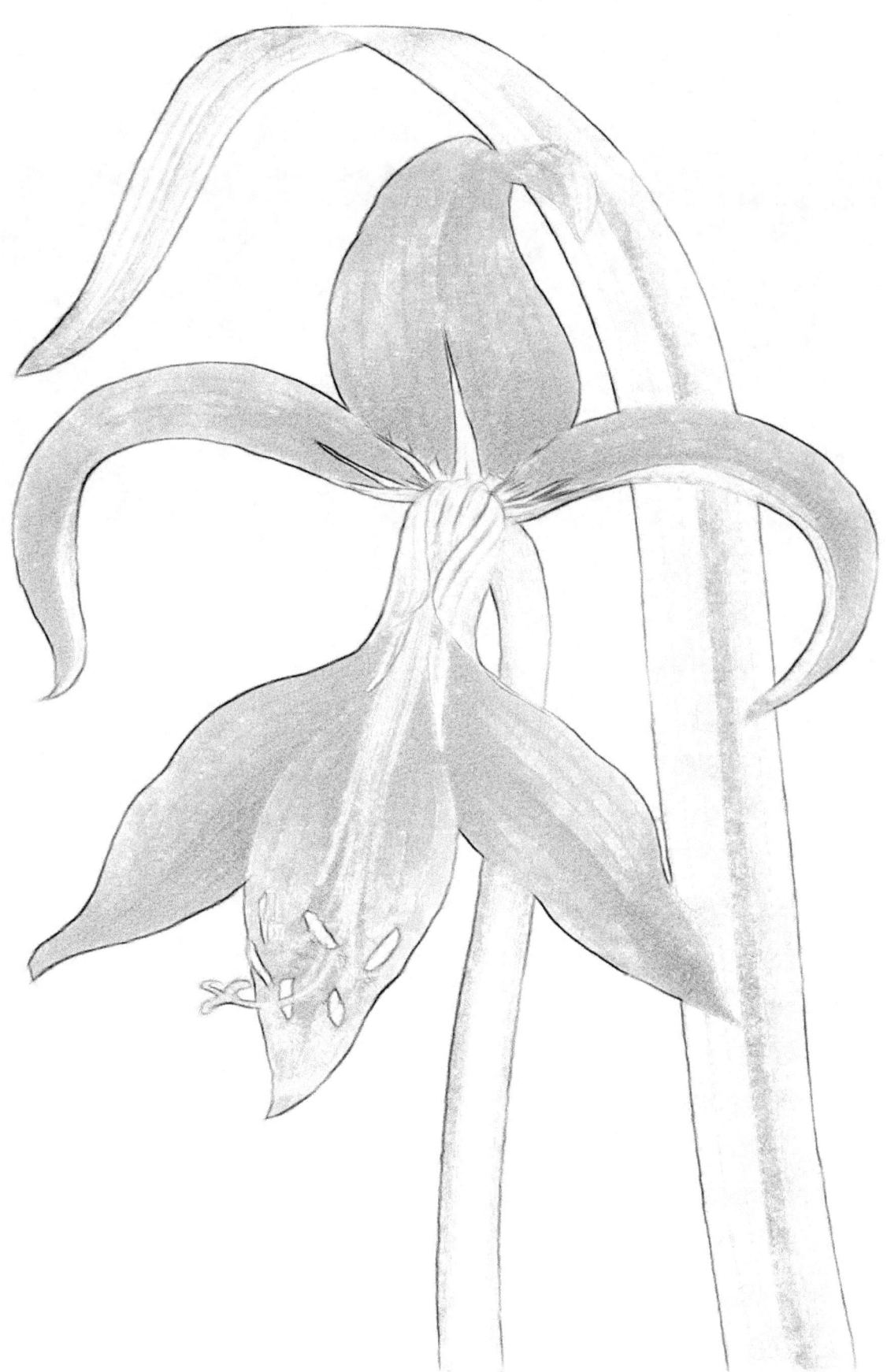

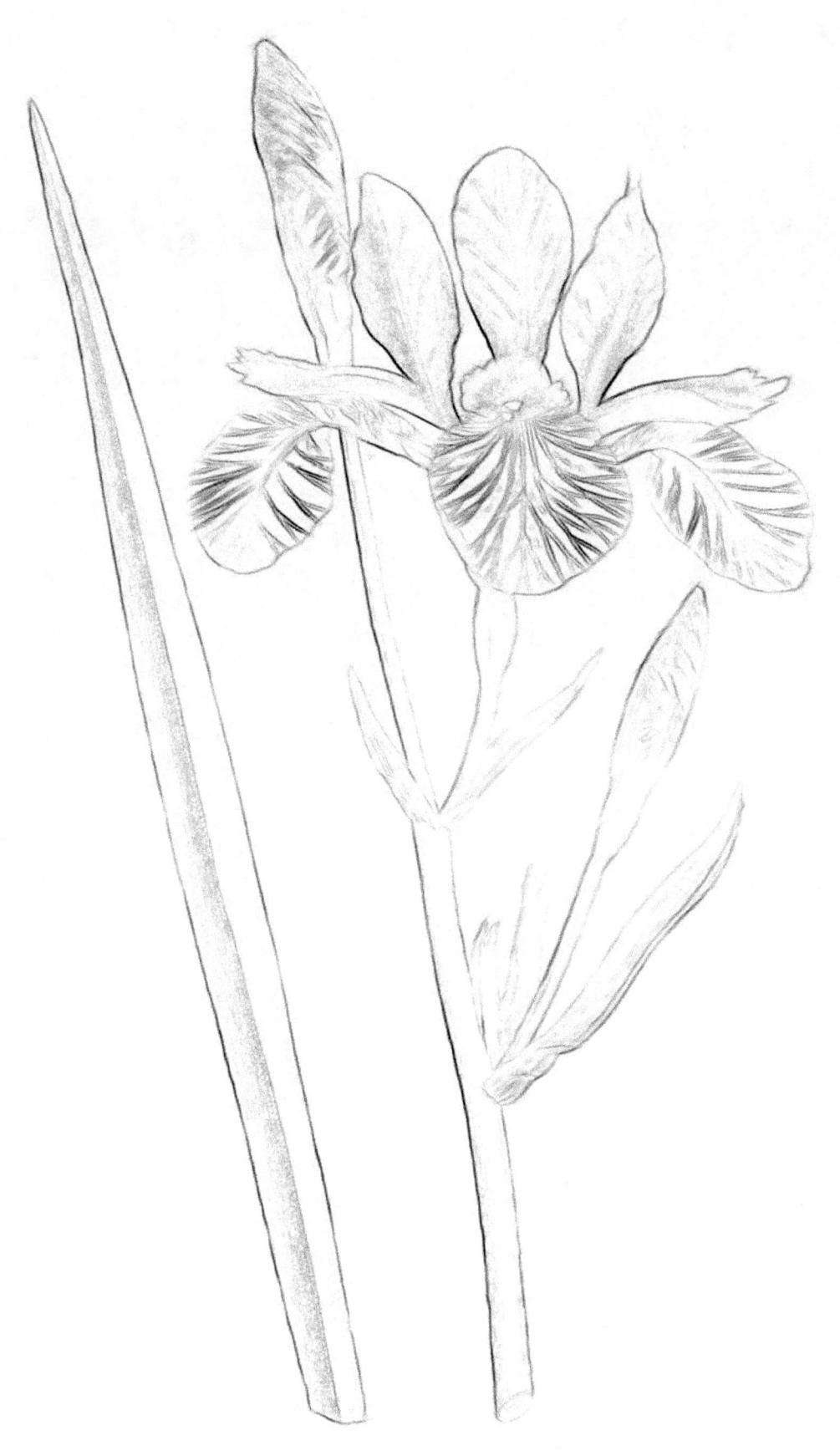

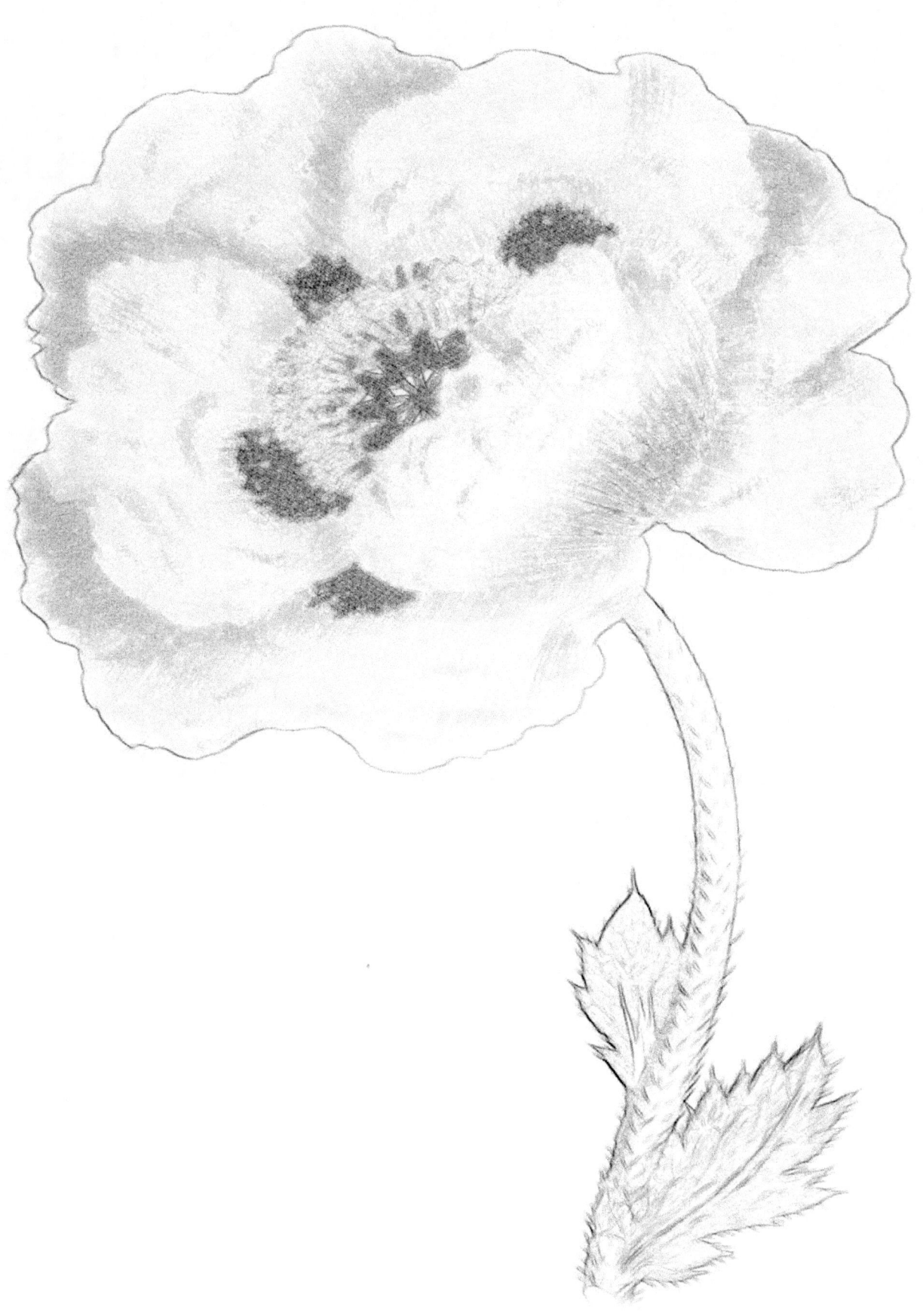

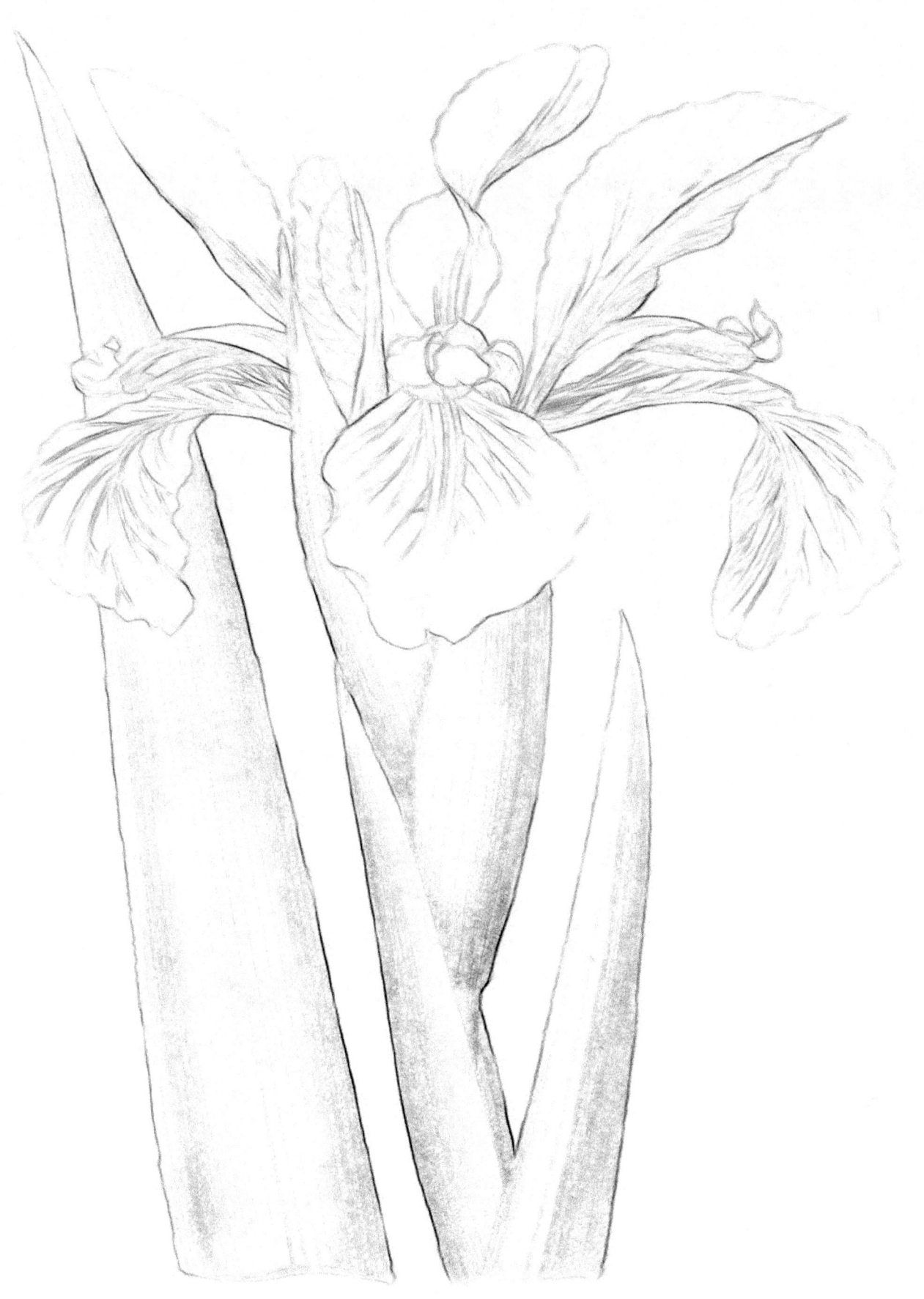

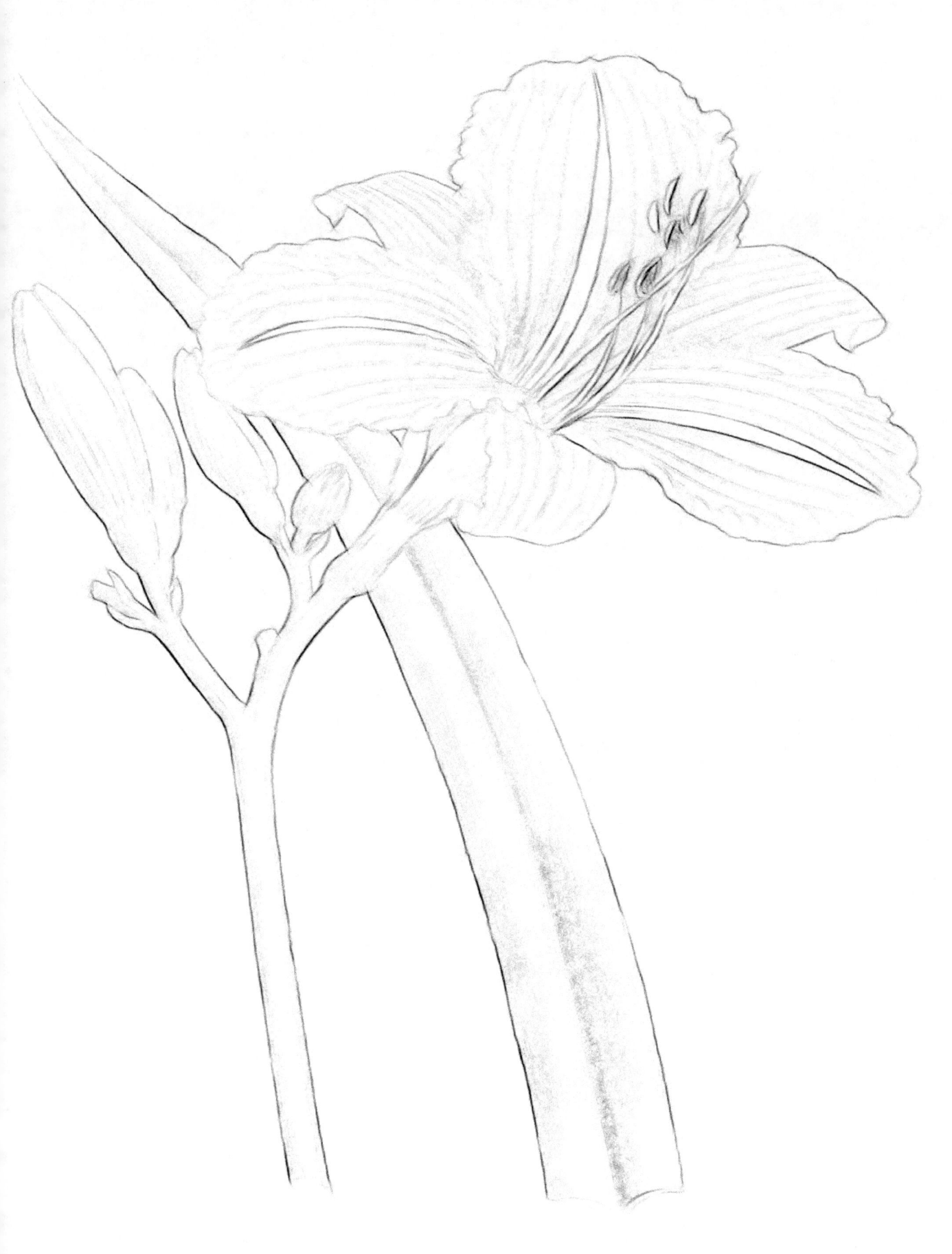

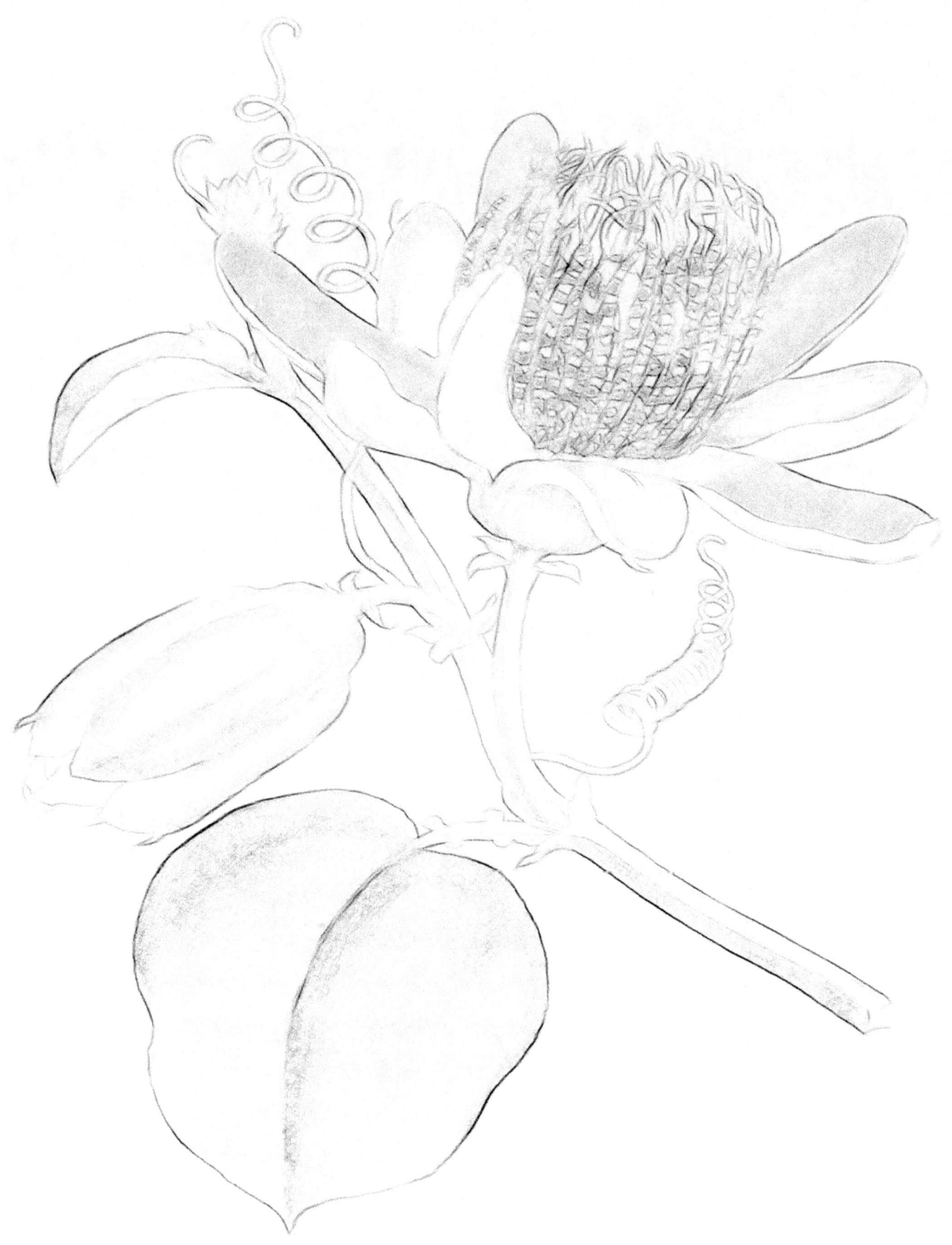

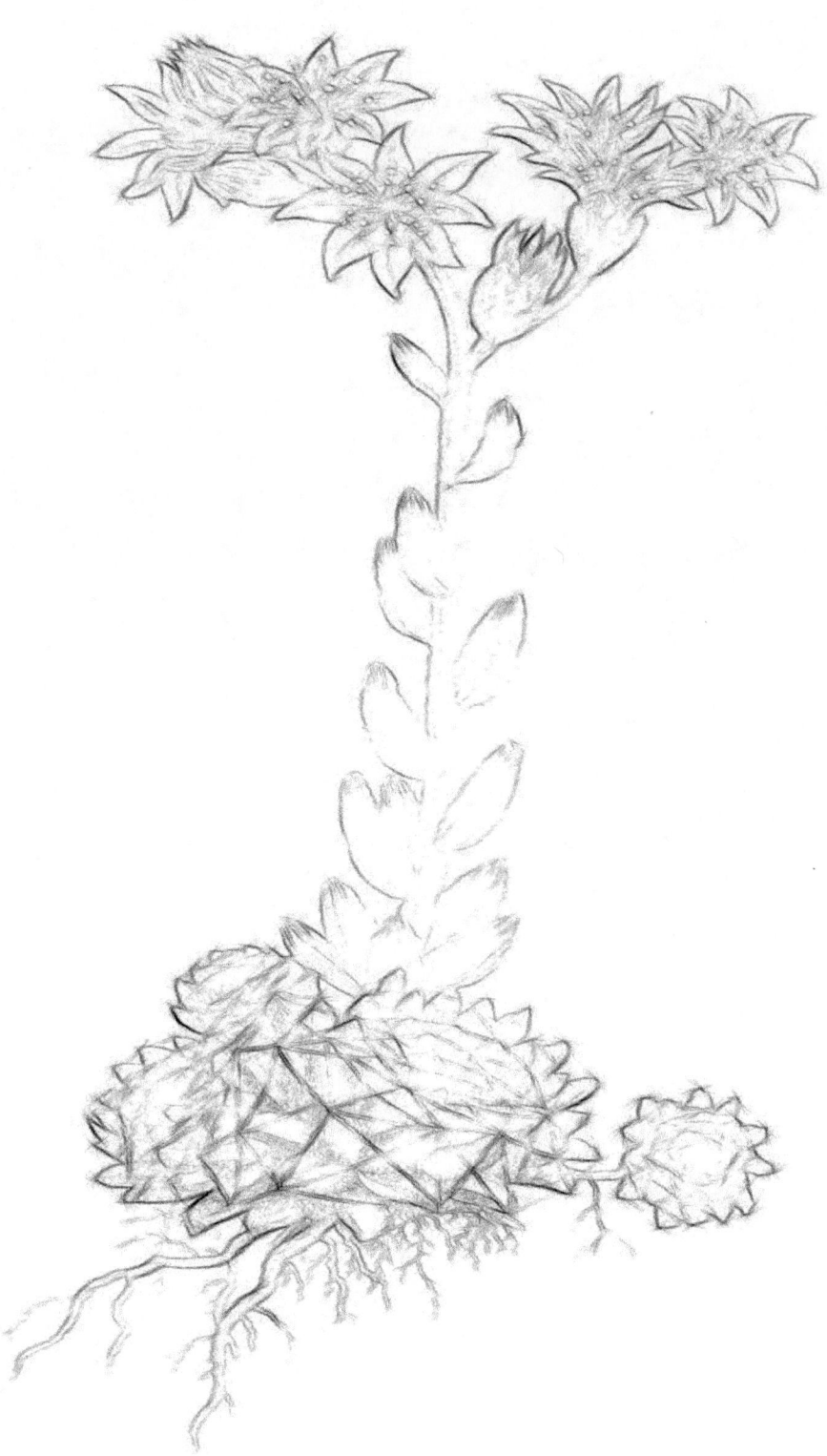

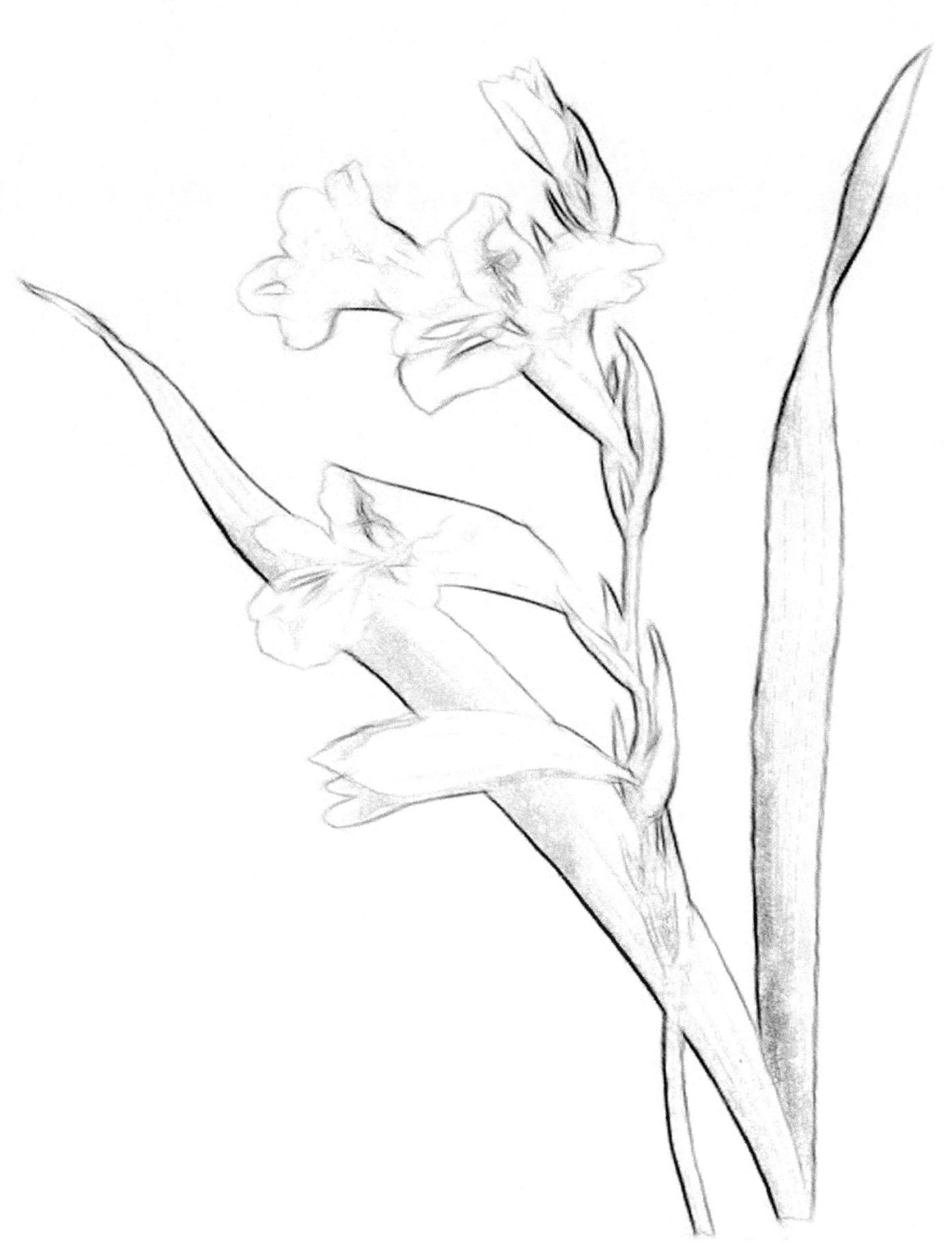

www.ingramcontent.com/pod-product-compliance
Lightning Source LLC
Chambersburg PA
CBHW080613180526
45168CB00007B/2899

* 9 7 8 1 5 1 1 8 7 8 8 5 2 *